101 Baby Item Patterns

For All Types of Crafts

Gail Forsyth

This publication has been designed so that the patterns can be used as templates for craft projects and you are free to use them for that purpose.

The book itself is not to be copied without written permission from the publisher or author.

Breed Profiles Publishing
Cedar City, UT 84721

The Joys of Crafting

Within these pages you'll find over 100 different baby item patterns to use as a template for your projects.

By using some tracing paper and the proper tracing pencil, you can draw the patterns on just about any medium to make some terrific craft items. Ask at the craft store for the tracing items you may need for your projects.

By tracing many of the patterns backwards, you'll get double the images. This is perfect for bookends, matching pillows, quilts, wall hangings and more.

You can enlarge or shrink the baby item patterns to suit your projects.

The possibilities are just about endless and will bring you lots of joy, entertainment and compliments.

So let's get crafting!

Helpful Tips

1) Wash and iron your fabric before cutting, if recommended for your project.

2) Use sharp scissors for less hand fatigue.

3) Allow seam allowance for sewing, if needed.

4) Use sharp pins on fabric to prevent puckers and snags.

5) Use safety eye protection when using saws or other machinery.

6) When using paints, be sure to ventilate the work area.

7) Don't use rusty pins on fabric, as this could leave marks.

8) Allow for the blade width, if using a saw on wood plastics, metal or glass. You may want to cut your patterns a little bigger.

9) Add or subtract the finer details on your patterns to fit your project.

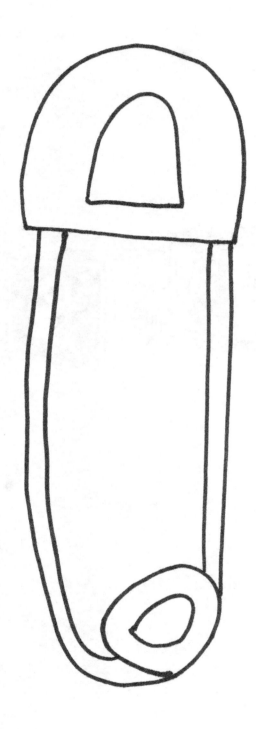

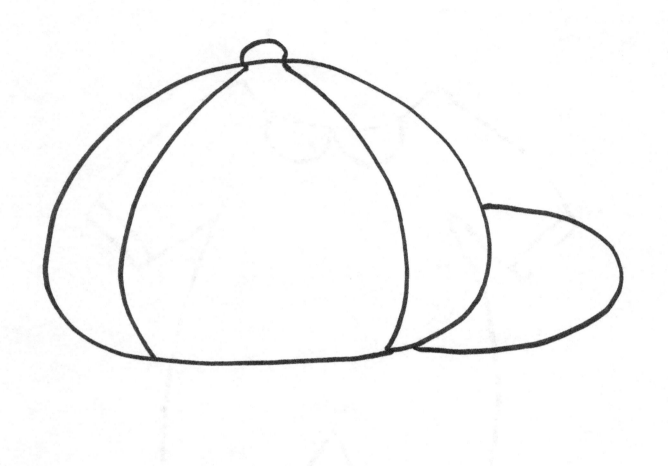

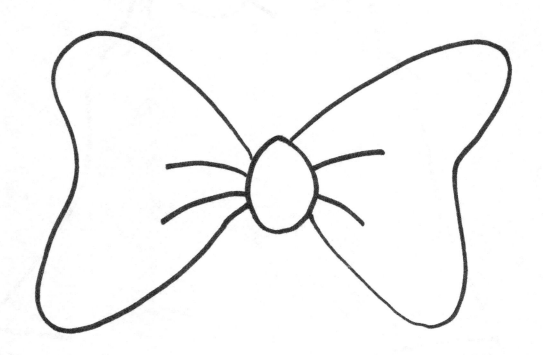

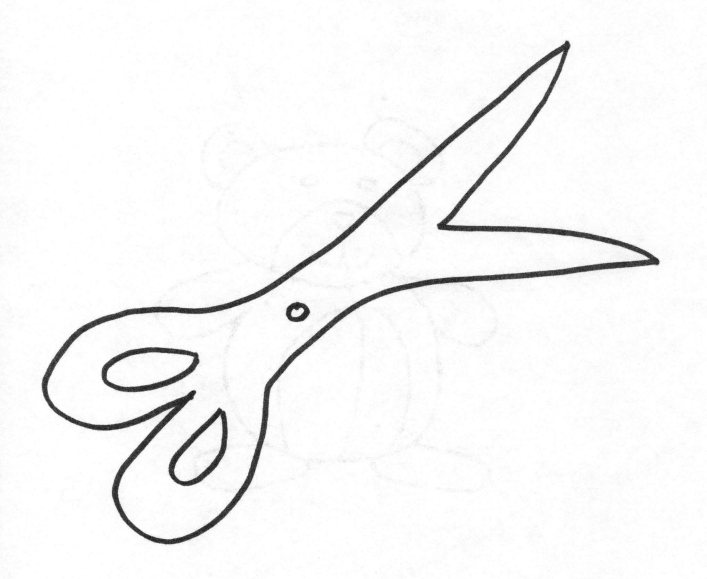

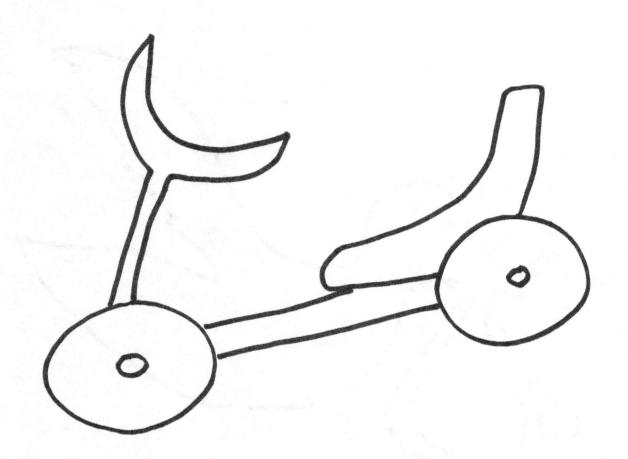

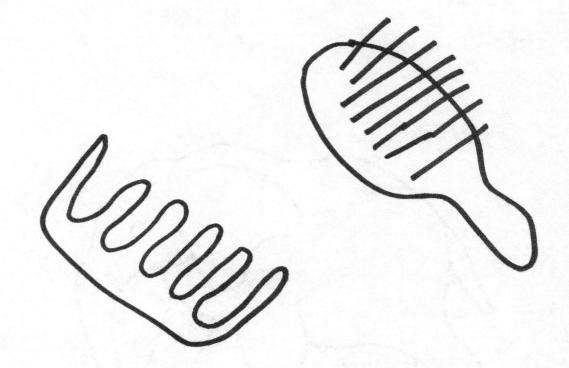

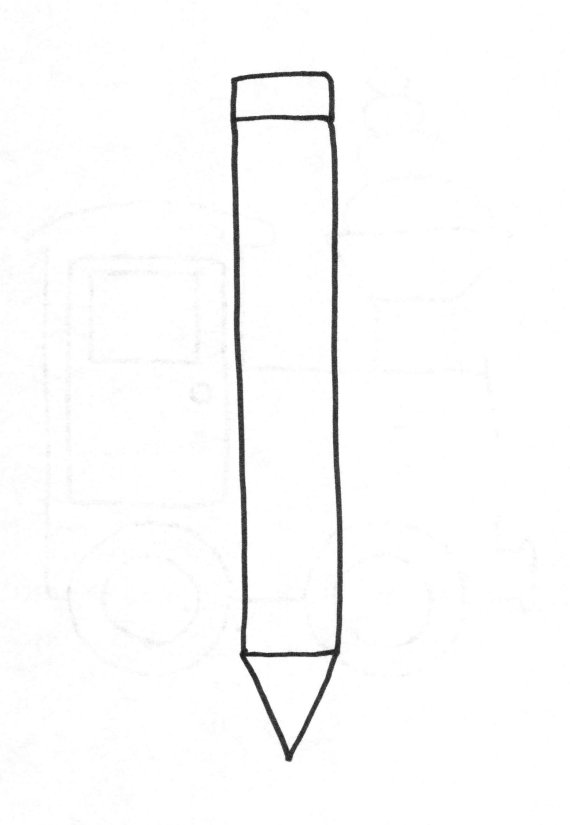

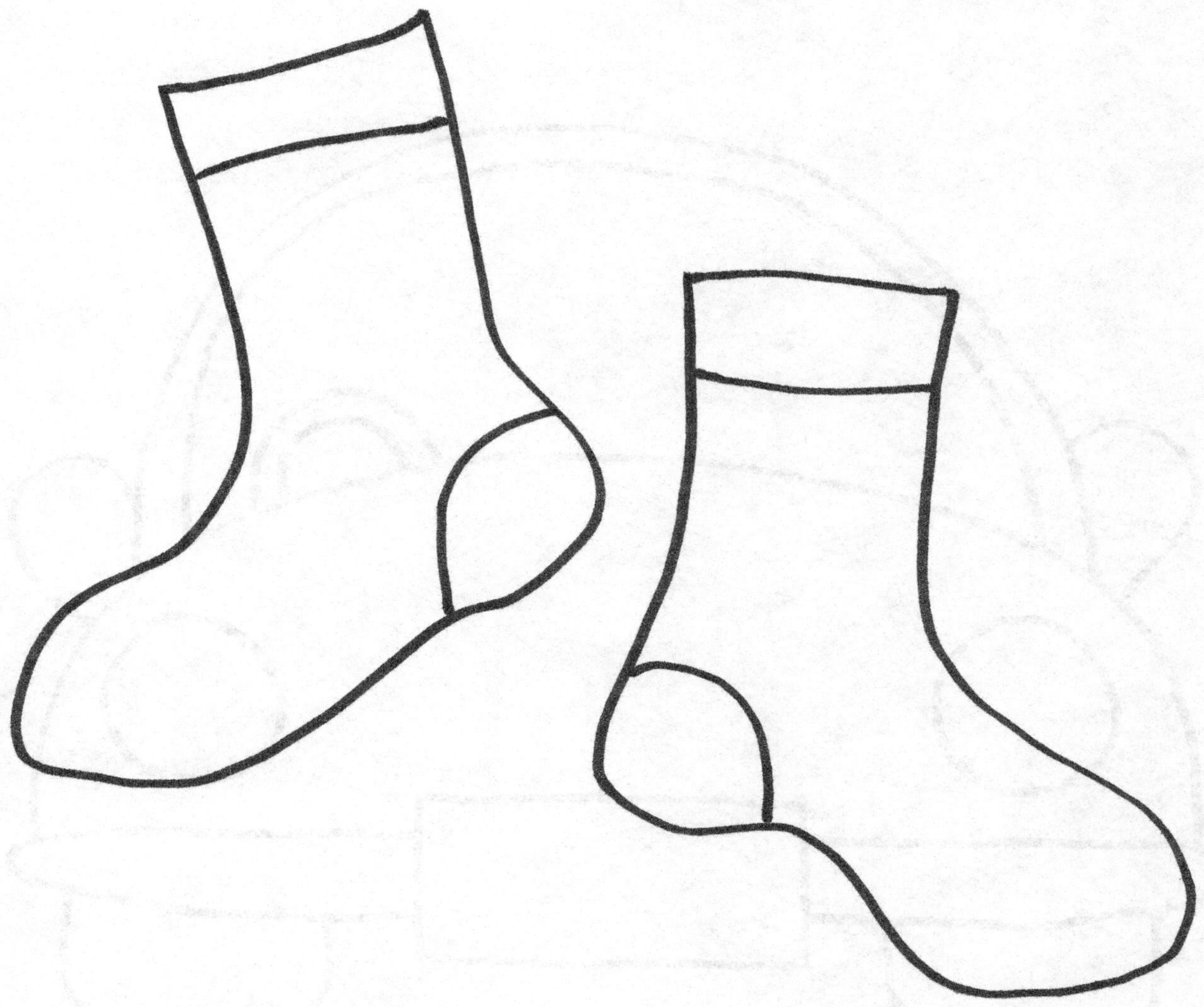

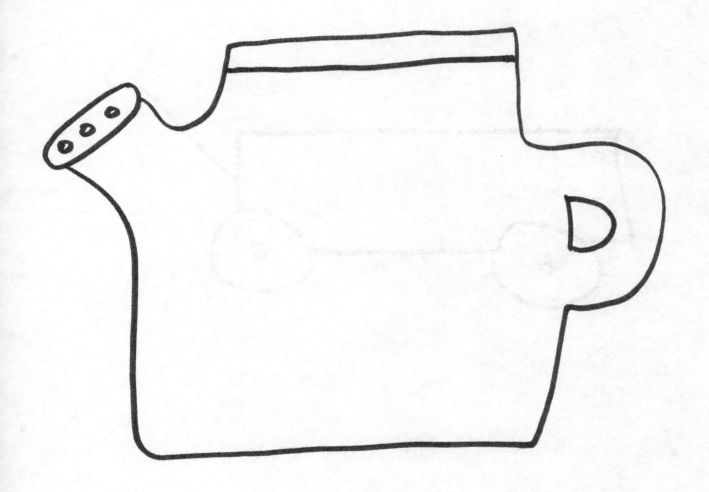

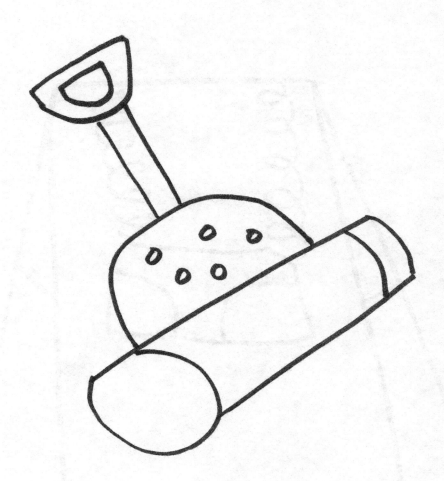

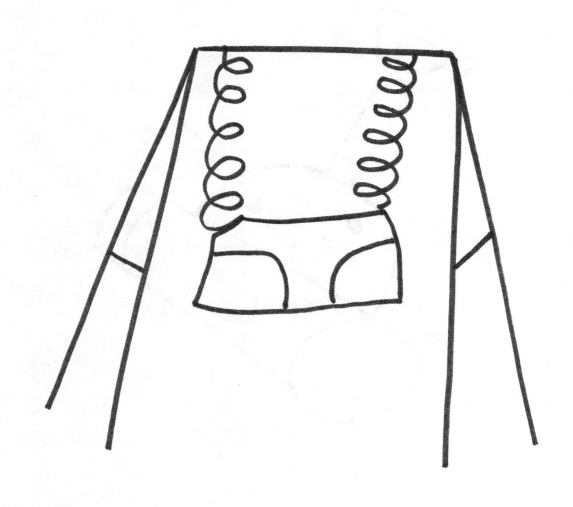

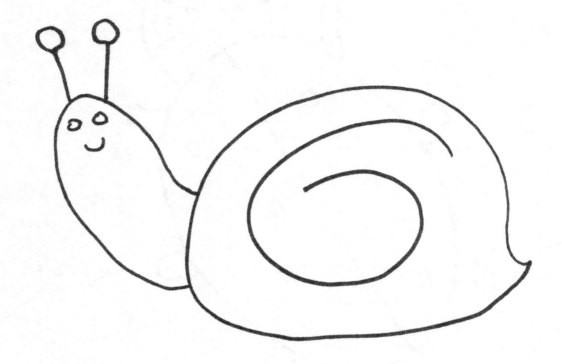

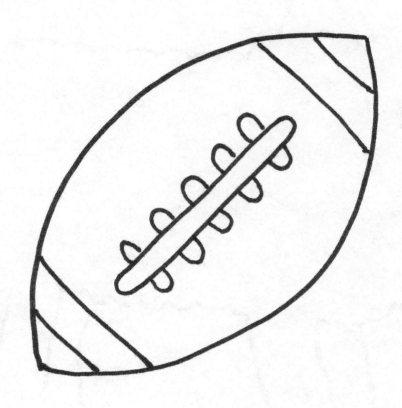

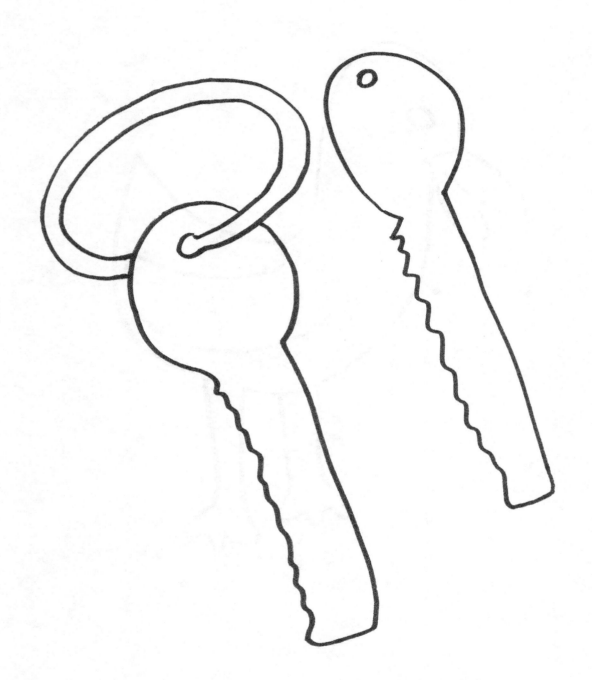

GIRL

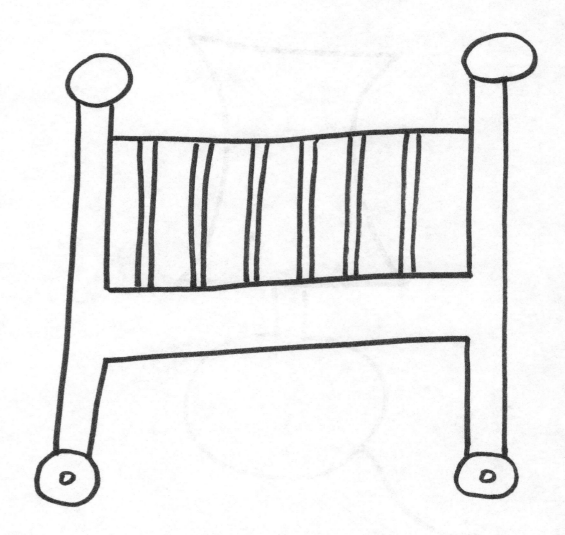

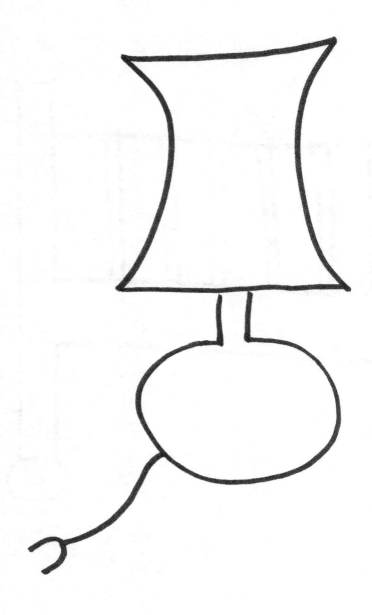

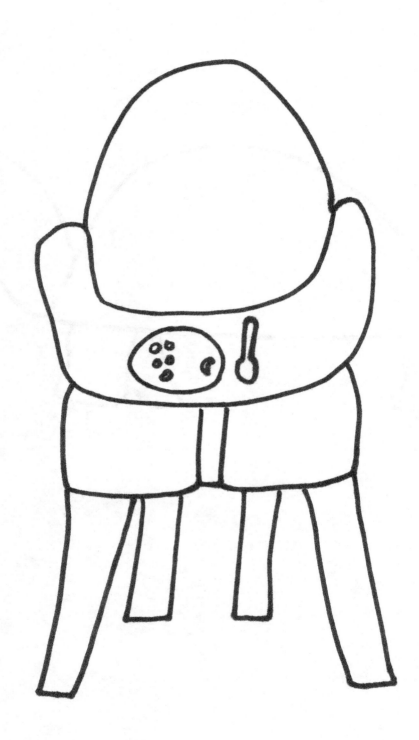

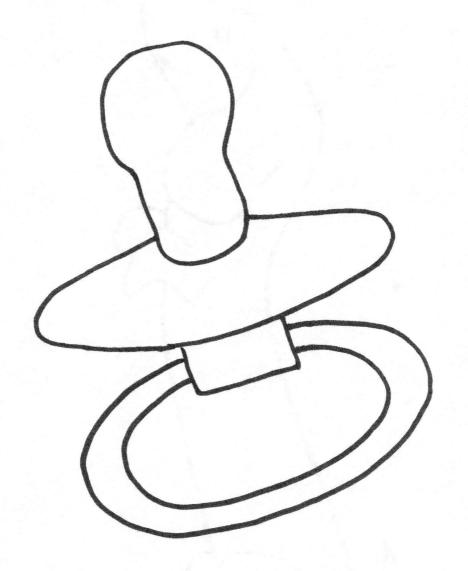

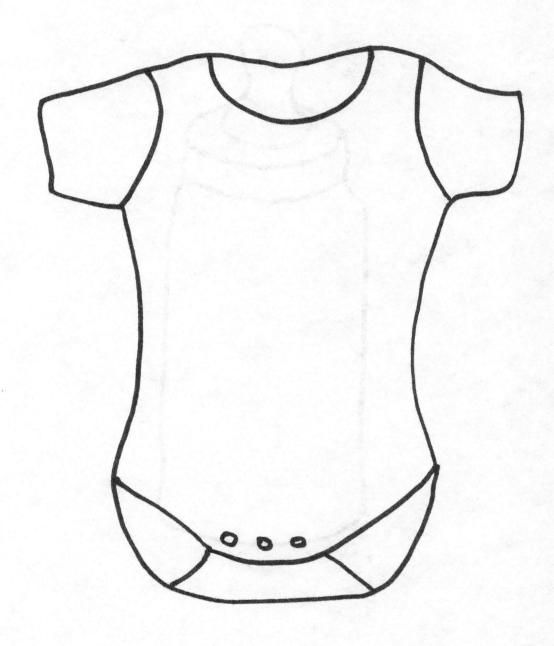

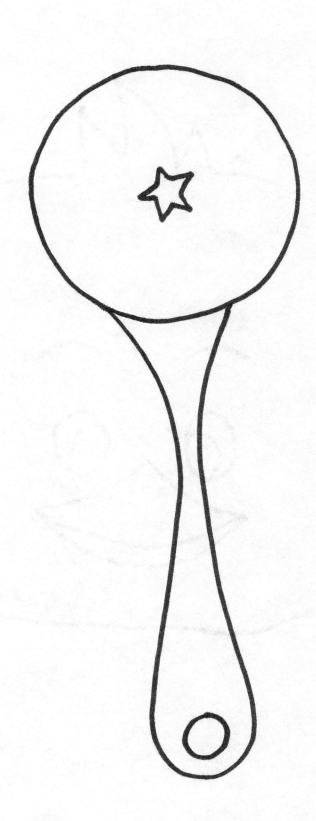

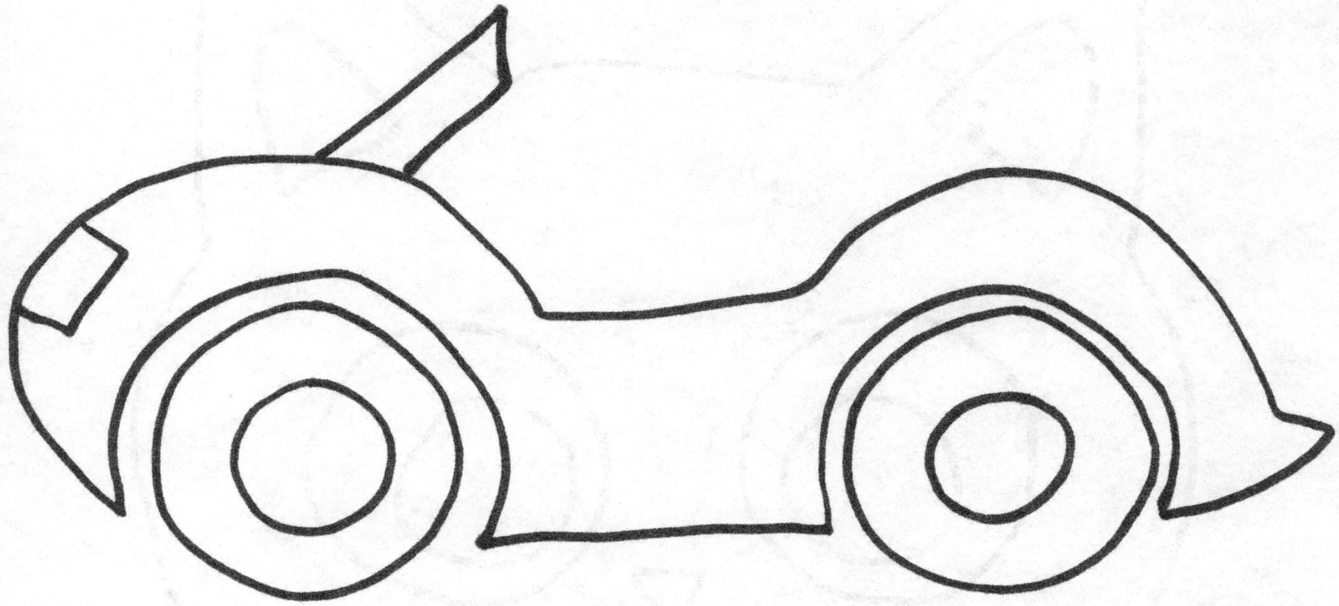

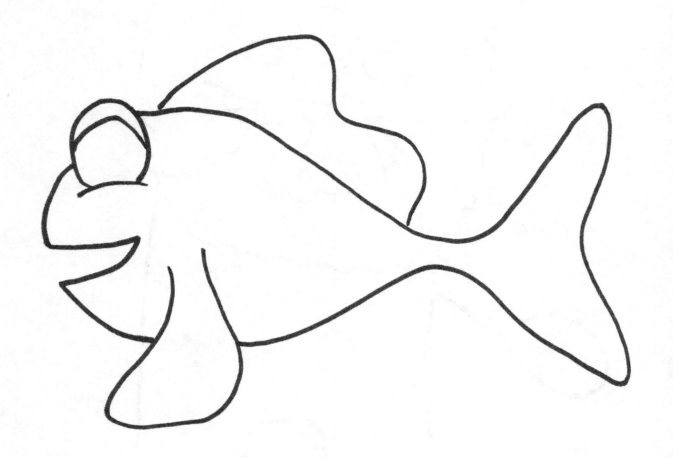

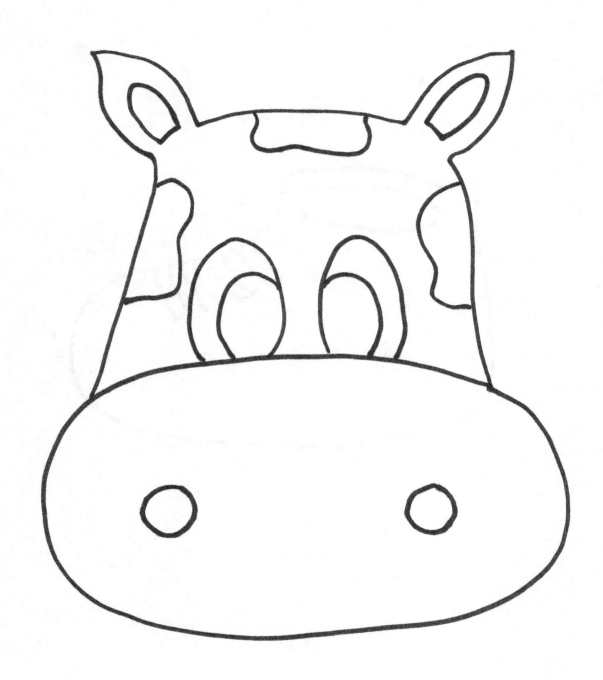

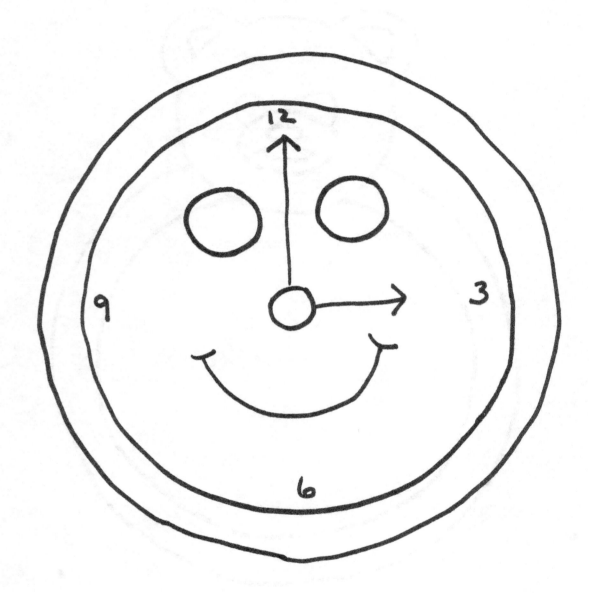

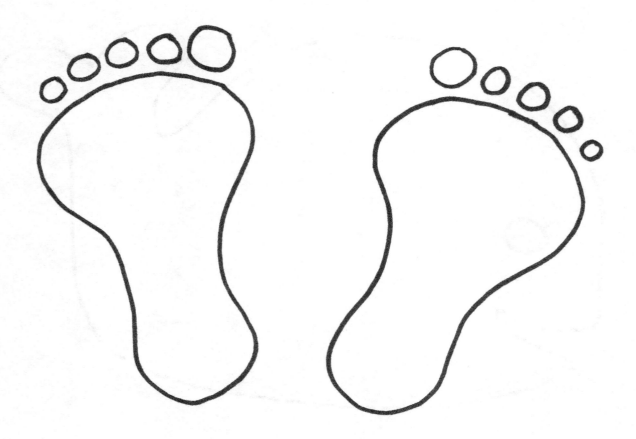

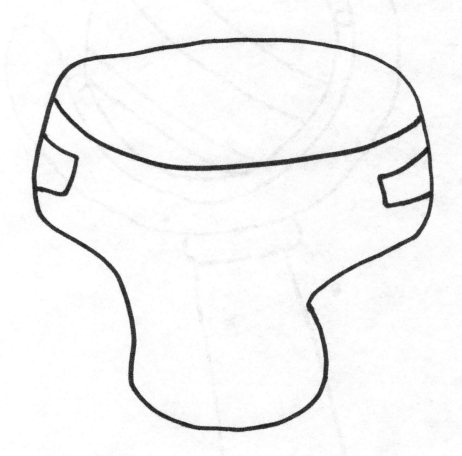

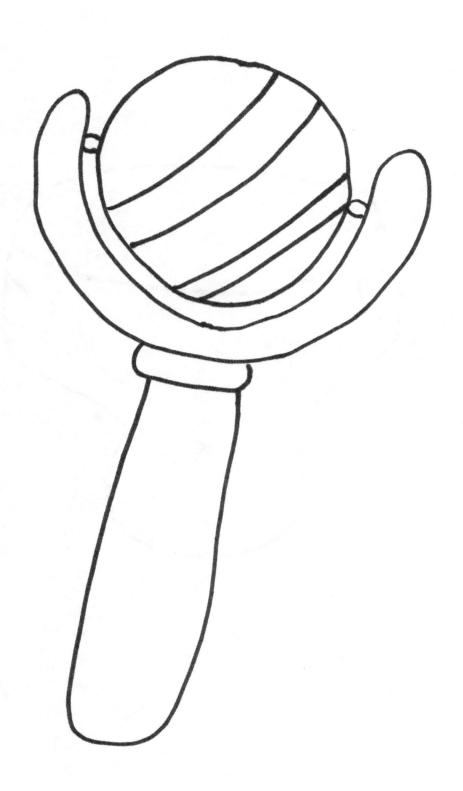

More Crafting Books

Looking for more inspiration for craft projects?

Collect the series of craft books below.

Ask for them from your favorite bookseller.

101 Dog Patterns

101 Baby Item Patterns

101 Assorted Animal Patterns

101 Holiday Patterns

Authored by Gail Forsyth

Made in the USA
Monee, IL
23 May 2025